Life
Changing
World
Changing

Prayer

Releasing God's Kingdom In Our World Today

By
Paul & Nuala O'Higgins

Life Changing, World Changing Prayer
© 2013 Paul & Nuala O'Higgins
ISBN 1494929074
and ISBN 9781494929077All rights reserved
Published by Reconciliation Outreach Inc.
P.O. Box 2778 Stuart, FL 34995
www.reconciliationoutreach.net

Table Of Contents

INTRODUCTION

Of all the abilities God has given to His children none is more wonderful than the amazing gift of prayer. Through this gift we can contact God's Presence, embrace His will, and bring His activity into our world. Prayer is the most important of all life skills, yet few of us receive any training in it. The aim of this book is to help us harness this infinite resource to more effectively change our lives and world.

We deal here with the practice and ministry of prayer. Our aim is to help equip a billion believers to function in the ministry of prayer and so bring God's will more fully into their lives and nations.

Almost every person prays. But not all pray effectively. Some do not know the difference between prayer and wishing. In this book we shall examine some of the rules of engagement of prayer that make it effective, easy and life changing. We shall also look at different dimensions and spheres of prayer.

Because many people associate prayer with religiosity, practical people often neglect to harness the effectiveness and power of prayer in their lives.

Chapter 1

Keys For Victorious Prayer

Prayer is the lifting up of our hearts and minds to the Most High God to e*mbrace His will* and bring His action and loving intervention into our lives.

In approaching God in payer we are not haphazard. There are *several keys* for victorious prayer through which God can be approached and His help received.

KEY I
Our Prayer Must Be To God Himself

When we talk about prayer it is important that we know to whom we are praying. Are we praying to The Most High God or to one of the lesser entities that exist in the spiritual unseen realm? The Bible reveals that The Most High God who created the universe and us made us to know Him, to love Him and serve Him. This also means He made us to communicate with Him and to reciprocate His love, by hearing Him and responding to Him.

"And I will give them a heart to know me, that I am the LORD: and they shall be my people, and I will be their God: for they shall return unto me with their whole heart." (Jer. 24:7)

Quoting the scriptures, Jesus said*: "You shall love the Lord your God with all your heart, and with all your soul, and with all your mind. This is the great and first commandment. And the second is like unto it, Thou shalt love thy neighbor as thyself."* (Mt 22: 37-38)

God does not want to be remote and distant from us. He wants us to be intimately *involved in every detail of our lives*. He wants us to have a living relationship with Him.

Since there are other spiritual forces, and personalities in the universe besides God, we need to be careful that when we pray we make our prayer to *God the Creator and Redeemer* who has made us for Him.

Because of guilt associated with sin, millions of people are fearful of approaching God directly. They are alienated from Him and ignorant of how to be reconciled to Him through faith in the all-sufficient atoning sacrifice of Jesus. They believe in His existence but have no personal relationship with Him. Because of this alienation and ignorance, they often express their need for worship by contacting other spirits.

God is a *"jealous God."* He knows the harm that comes when we come under the influence of other spirits. Often these spirits masquerade as angels of light and liberation, when in fact they have the exactly opposite effect, because they draw us away from the care of God the Father.

John warned against this when he wrote: *"Beloved, do not believe every spirit, but test the spirits to see whether they are of God; for many false prophets have gone out into the world. By this you know the Spirit of God: every spirit which confesses that Jesus Christ has come in the flesh is of God, and every spirit which does not confess Jesus is not of God. This is the spirit of antichrist, of which you heard that it was coming, and now it is in the world already."* (1 John 4:1- 3)

Believers therefore should be careful to make their prayer to God the Father through Jesus the Messiah. We worship the God revealed in the pages of the Bible - God the Creator and the Redeemer. In today's multi-cultural world the name "God" is ascribed to many spirits. Hindus worship tens of thousands of gods. These are spirits of the unseen realm whose influence they invoke to help them with life's problems. Many Muslims also have a distorted view of the personality, character and nature of God which they have received from traditions which distort the true picture of God. Whenever they pray to a god that is hostile to the people who follow the biblical view of God they are in fact praying to another god who is not the true God. Others regard God as the life force of nature or the powers of the soul that lie within us all. They then pray to this cosmic energy and are not really praying to Almighty God.

"Our God is in the heavens; He does whatever He pleases. Their idols are silver and gold, the work of men's hands. They have mouths, but do not speak; eyes, but do not see. They have ears, but do not hear; noses, but do not smell. They have hands, but do not feel; feet, but do not walk; and they do not make a sound in their throat. Those who make them are like them; so are all who trust in them."* (Psalm 115 1-8)

Millions today contact psychics and fortunetellers. In many cases they think that they are simply engaging in a harmless game but they are in fact contacting oppressing spirits.

Prayer can be compared to a letter which must be addressed to the right person at the right address - The Creator God, The Most High God who rules the Universe with His Son through the Holy Spirit. So all prayer must be addressed to

- the One true God
- the God of the Bible
- the God of Abraham. Isaac and Jacob
- the God and Father of Our Lord Jesus Christ
- the God who has revealed Himself in the Bible and in His saving acts in history

Any spirit that does not recognize His exclusive claim and His supreme authority is illegal. Therefore prayer made to any other spirit (though it may be sincere) is not going to reach its destination.

God warns us not to pray to any other God than Himself. (Exodus 20:3) We are not to pray to angels, saints or any other spirit except to the only true God who rules the universe.

Many mistakenly make their prayers to Mary the mother of Jesus, because they lack confidence in their own prayers and ability to come boldly before the Lord through the Blood of Jesus. They rely on her to 'mediate' their prayer. However, the scripture states that Jesus is the only Meditator between God and man. (1 Tim. 2:5) His Atonement opened up a direct access to God for all who come through Him. Those who admire and esteem Mary do well, but when they pray to her they dishonor her mission as the mother of the Mediator and violate the message of the gospel.

"I am the LORD your God, who brought you out of the land of Egypt, out of the house of bondage. "You shall have no other gods before me. You shall not make for yourself a graven image, or any likeness of anything that is in heaven above, or that is in the earth beneath, or that is in the water under the earth; you shall not bow down to them or serve them; for I the LORD your God am a jealous God." (Exodus 20:2-4)

Jesus, seeing the profound thirst for spiritual truth that we humans have, came to rescue us from the oppression of fallen and false spirits. Only He brings us into direct contact and relationship with His loving Father our Creator. From this place of restoration we enter into the realm of true prayer.

He said, *"I am the way the truth and the Life, No one comes to the Father except by me."* (John 14:1) He also said *"The thief comes to steal kill and destroy but I am come that you may have life and have it more abundantly."* (John 10:10)

True prayer is for those who place themselves under God's protection. It is for those who recognize the existence of the creator God and His power to intervene lovingly in their lives, as they approach Him though the blood of Jesus. So when we pray we must pray to the real God and not to some fallen spirit.

We have seen above that there are many spirits in the universe but only one true God. Prayer to God must be made to God Himself and not to any other entity or projection of our imagination.

KEY II
Pray To The Father Through Jesus

The Atoning Sacrifice of Jesus is the central fact of history. It revolutionizes prayer as it removes the barriers between God and us - the blame, judgment and condemnation of our sin, sins and guilt. This allows us to approach Him with confidence.

"Therefore, my brothers, having boldness to enter into the Holy of Holies by the blood of Jesus, by a new and living way which He has consecrated for us through

the veil, that is to say, His flesh; and having a High Priest over the house of God, let us draw near with a true heart in full assurance of faith, having our hearts sprinkled from an evil conscience and our bodies having been washed with pure water." (Hebrews 10:19-22)

Prayer made on the basis of the atoning sacrifice of Jesus changes the way we pray forever and brings our prayer to a level of authority and effectiveness that was not previously possible.

The Bible reveals that though sin had separated us from God, the Atoning Sacrifice of Jesus has restored our access to God. The Temple sacrifices, and the Passover ritual reveal that we must base our approach to God on the Atoning Sacrifice.

KEY III
Pray In Line With The Interests Of The Kingdom

Jesus taught us to pray *"Thy Kingdom come."* The plan of God is to cover the earth with the blessedness, glory and joy of His Kingdom. His kingdom is not a kingdom of slavery and coercion, - it is a kingdom of love, joy and freedom. When we pray, we should be careful to pray **according to the word of God and the will of God.** It is obviously ridiculous to ask God to do something that is contrary to His will. In the scriptures God has revealed His will so that we can pray in line with His written word i.e. in line with His will.

His word contains prophecies, promises, and precepts. Prophecy reveals God's plan, the promises reveal God's benefits and the precepts reveal God's standards.

Our prayer then is not a mere projection of our wishes but an intelligent cooperation with the will of God. Those who pray in line with the word of God pray with authority and confidence. Knowledge of the word of God is key to effective prayer. The revelation of the word of God throughout the world is the most important factor in elevating mankind from the sorry condition into which we have descended.

The revelation of God's will, expressed in His word, enables all men to pray accurately. It is presumptuous to claim Bible promises to suit ourselves and so try to impose our will on God. Such prayer is not in the spirit - it is merely an exercise of psychic (soul) force. Real prayer discerns God's will and confidently prays it through.

James explains that many prayers go unanswered because we are praying for matters that are not aligned with God's will.

"You desire and do not have; so you kill. And you covet and cannot obtain; so you fight and wage war. You do not have, because you do not ask. You ask and do not receive, because you ask wrongly, to spend it on your passions." (James 4:2-3)

Before we pray it is wise to

- humble ourselves
- quieten our opinions
- seek God's face and will
- and then pray confidently.

KEY IV
Asking In Jesus' Name

"Therefore, brethren, since we have confidence to enter the sanctuary by the blood of Jesus, by the new and living way which He opened for us through the curtain, that is, through his flesh, and since we have a great priest over the house of God, let us draw near with a true heart in **full assurance of faith, with** *our hearts sprinkled clean from an evil conscience and our bodies washed with pure water."* (Hebrews 10:19-21)

In the days of the Temple, priests approached God only after they had purified themselves and had put off their own garments and put on special linen garments designated by God.

As we approach God through Jesus, who is our great and eternal High Priest, we approach God in the name of Jesus. As He was about to go to Calvary, Jesus instructed His followers on the incredible access to God's presence and power in prayer that this would give them.

"Whatever you ask **in my name**, *I will do it, that the Father may be glorified in the Son; if you ask anything*

in my name, *I will do it."* (Jn. 14:13-14)

"In that day you will ask nothing of me. Truly, truly, I say to you, if you ask anything of the Father, He will give it to you in my name. Hitherto you have asked nothing ***in my name****; ask, and you will receive, that your joy may be full."* (John 16:23-24)

He gave us the right to use His Name in prayer. We, who once were estranged from God, have been given a high privilege with God so that we can pray in the Name of Jesus. False humility and human tradition, has robs us of our authority in prayer.

The Name of Jesus is a privilege that can be exercised by believers since Jesus' Ascension. He spoke to His disciples about a kind of prayer that they could use *"in that day."* (*John 16:23*) Prayer in the Name of Jesus was unknown until the days of the New Covenant. It is a totally new kind of prayer made possible through His Ascension. It is the unique privilege of the believers in Him. *"In that day"* refers to the days that follow His Ascension and return in triumph to the right hand of the Father. *"Therefore God also has highly exalted Him and given Him the name which is above every name, that at* ***the name of Jesus*** *every knee should bow, of those* ***in heaven****, and of those* ***on earth****, and of those* ***under the earth****..."* (Phil. 2:9-11)

Praying **in the Name of Jesus** is an unique privilege of genuine disciples of Jesus *"In that day you will ask in My name, and I do not say to you* *that I shall pray the Father for you; for the Father Himself loves you, because you have loved Me, and have believed that I came forth from God."* (John 16:26-27)

*" If ye shall ask any thing **in my name**, I will do it."* (John 14:14) It is the legal right of those who have come into union with Jesus through the New Birth and the New Covenant to act and pray in His name and for His purposes.

When Peter healed the man at the gate of the Temple He explained that the healing came about not through His piety but through the use of the name of Jesus who gave His disciples the right to pray and minister in His name. "*Men of Israel, why do you marvel at this? Or why look so intently at us, as though by our own power or godliness we had made this man walk? The God of Abraham, Isaac, and Jacob, the God of our fathers, glorified His Servant Jesus ... **and His name, through faith in His name**, has made this man strong, whom you see and know. Yes, the faith which comes through Him has given him this perfect soundness in the presence of you all."* (Acts 3:12, 13,16)

In prayer and ministry we rely not on our piety but on the fact that we are in united with Jesus and have the privilege of using the power of His name.

Key V
Ask

Many people presume that God's blessing

and purposes will *automatically* come to pass. They think that if God wants to do something He will do it with or without our cooperation in prayer. This seems pious, holy and religious, but it is not true. God cannot rule in this world without our prayer. To do so would be to bypass the He has given to us, and turn us into robots. He wants us to engage our free will with His revealed will.

In this way His will and power will be released in the world. This is basis of the awesome power, authority and privilege of prayer Unless we ask, God's hand is hindered from bringing His purposes to pass in our lives and His blessings into our situations.

Another factor that hinders us from asking is making the assumption that the matters we are asking about are *too small for God*. This is an insult to the loving nature of God and to His fatherly concern with everything about us. He is concerned with *"even the hairs of our heads."* Not a sparrow falls to the ground without His noticing. (Mt. 10 -30-31)

To object that He has far bigger problems than ours to take care of and that it would be selfish to ask Him to concern Himself with our interests is to fail to realize what a loving Father He is. God who created and controls the universe with its vast galaxies is also the One who created the atom and the sub atomic particle. He can handle the big picture and the microscopic picture with the same ease.

God really does invite us to pray about every little concern as well as the greater matters of His kingdom.

"The Lord is at hand. Be careful for nothing; but in every thing by prayer and supplication with thanksgiving let your requests be made known unto God. And the peace of God, which passes all understanding, shall keep your hearts and minds through Christ Jesus." (Phil. 4:6-7)

KEY VI
Believe

"Therefore I tell you, whatever you ask in prayer, believe that you have received it, and it will be yours." (Mark 11:24)

It is really not difficult to believe that your prayer is answered when you know you are praying in line with God's will. You are simply opening up your heart to receive what God has already promised to give.

Our heavenly Father does not have to give each of us a mere six billionth of His attention. All of His attention is on each of us all the time. We cannot do that but God can. So when you go to pray to Him you have all of His attention!

There is often a time lapse between the making of a prayer and its answer. To keep our faith active during a time lapse, we simply thank God that He has heard the prayer and is answering it. Jesus prayed before Lazarus tomb

19

"Father I know you always hear (when I pray)." (John 11:41) We too can have this same confidence.

There is of course a mystery in prayer .. that we will never fully understand in this present age. It will remain a mystery (which no amount of theological explanation can make clear) why many prayers, which are undoubtedly in line with God's will, seem to remain unanswered. We know when God's kingdom finally triumphs on the earth everything that blocks His will being done will be removed and every promise will be fulfilled. In the meantime all believers live in a partial fulfillment of God's highest and best purposes for our lives. Yet even though we do not see everything fulfilled, every disease healed, every flaw in our personalities removed, we still contend in faith. *"Not that I have already obtained this or am already perfect; but I press on to make it my own, because Christ Jesus has made me his own."* (Phil 3:12) We keep pressing on in faith and prayer to see more and more of God's will fulfilled in every aspect of our lives.

KEY VII
Forgive

"And whenever you stand praying, forgive, if you have anything against any one; so that your Father also who is in heaven may forgive you your trespasses." (Mark 11:25)

Life Changing, World Changing Prayer

Much of Jesus' teaching was devoted to the subject of forgiveness. We who have been forgiven everything by God must live in the realm of total forgiveness. To do this we not only receive forgiveness but also give forgiveness.

If we do not forgive neither will our heavenly Father forgive us. When we do not forgive we cut off the flow of God's mercies and blessings to us. It is a waste of time to go through the motions of prayer if we have any unforgiveness towards anyone.

This means that we forgive everyone of every real or imagined thing they have done against us, including parents, teachers, employers, politicians , members of other religions etc. etc.

It is equally important to forgive ourselves. People often use phrases such as: "I can never forgive myself for.' "I am mad at myself." "I am so stupid." " I hate my looks" etc. etc. These kinds of statements indicate self-hatred, self-bitterness and unforgiveness toward self and they certainly block the flow to answered prayer.

To forgive ourselves we acknowledge our past sins and mistake, then totally and fully receive God's forgiveness (on the basis that Jesus bore them) and then consciously extend this forgiveness to ourselves. God can take the past and redeem it when we release it to Him.

"And we know that all things work together for good to those who love God, to those who are called according to His purpose." (Rom 8:28) He will make it better that the bad thing happened than I if it had never happened. In light of this it becomes easy to forgive.

Forgiving does not mean that we agree with, or think it wrong to disagree with the person we are forgiving. It simply means that we release the person from all ill will or animosity towards them in our hearts, and ask God to bless and change them.

Joseph did this when he said to his brothers who had mistreated him. *"As for you, you meant evil against me;"* he said *"but God meant it for good, that many people should be kept alive."*(Gn. 50:20)

When we do likewise, we forgive from the heart. In the parable of the unjust steward, Jesus shows that God requires this of us. We who have been released from so great a debt of sin must also release those who have offended us. (Matt. 18:35)

Key VIII
Ask The Holy Spirit's Help

"Likewise the Spirit also helps our infirmities. For we do not know what we should pray for as we ought, but the Spirit Himself makes intercession for us with groanings which cannot be uttered." (Romans 8:26)

If God's will is not clear in a situation the Holy Spirit will guide our prayer. We can easily rush into prayer without thinking through what is the appropriate thing to pray. For example, it might be more appropriate to pray for someone to get some training rather than pray they get a job, or it may be wiser to pray for someone to learn contentment in their present situation than to pray that God changes it.

As we allow the Holy Spirit to direct, He can show the best way to pray in any given situation or point out a blockage to the answer of or prayers. He can give us a word of wisdom or a word of knowledge or a picture, which will unlock the situation. As we wait on Him and yield to Him He will guide us in our prayer so that we pray with a far greater precision and wisdom. In this way, prayer becomes part of a circle of receiving God's will within us and returning it to Him in prayer, so that it can be accomplished on earth.

KEY IX
Exercise Your Will

It is something we do, by a deliberate exercise of our will. Jesus said when you pray:

- *"Go into your inner room,"*
- *"Shut the door and"*
- *"Pray to your Father who is in the Secret place."*

- *"Your Father who sees in secret will reward openly."* (Matthew 6:6)

We deliberately go to a place of prayer. We shut the door on the world around us (including the sound of our own emotions, thoughts and distractions) and deliberately lay our requests before Our Heavenly Father. We are intentionally coming before God our Father knowing that He is real, that He loves us and that we need His help.

When we shut the door to the clamor of the world we can bring everything to Him.
In prayer we go to God in the secret place, having no secrets before Him, and ask Him to become involved.

Prayer is not simply having a stream of consciousness that somehow involves thoughts about God going through our mind. It is going to God formally, deliberately and consciously to transact holy business with Him. We shut the door. We make our requests to Him in secret and He will act openly. *"But you, when you pray, go into your room, and when you have shut your door, pray to your Father who is in the secret place; and your Father who sees in secret will reward you openly."* (Matt. 6:6)

Key X
Pray With Thanksgiving

Discouragement is one of the pitfalls that prayer warriors are prone to. The intercessor can easily become saddened and overburdened by the problems for which he is praying. This is why we must always pray from a position of victory and in a spirit of thanksgiving and praise – what a mighty God we serve!

"Make a joyful noise to the LORD, all the lands!
Serve the LORD with gladness!
Come into his presence with singing! Know that the LORD is God!
It is he that made us, and we are his; we are his people, and the sheep of his pasture.
Enter his gates with thanksgiving, and his courts with praise! Give thanks to him, bless his name!
For the LORD is good; his steadfast love endures for ever, and his faithfulness to all generations." (Psalm 100)

The garments of the priests are festal garments and so the attitude of the intercessor should be cheerful. We are celebrating God's goodness and mercy and drawing them into our situations. We are focusing not on the problems of the world but on the SOLUTION to the problems of the world. We are not praying under the burden but on the reverse side of the cross – seated with Him in the heavenlies –where all things are under His feet.

We should always remember that prayer is the joyful embracing of God's wonderful will and plan to alter the world with His goodness. Our prayer must be framed in thanksgiving to God for His willingness to involve Himself in our affairs.

"The Lord is at hand. Have no anxiety about anything, but in everything by prayer and supplication with thanksgiving let your requests be made known to God. And the peace of God, which passes all understanding, let your requests be made known to God. And the peace of God, which passes all understanding, will keep your hearts and minds in Christ Jesus" (Philippians 4:6)

CHAPTER 2

WORSHIP & AWE COME FIRST

The all sufficiency of the cross of Jesus has bridged the gap between God and man. We are no longer estranged or at a distance from Him. *"But now in Christ Jesus you who were once afar off are made near by the blood of Christ."* (Eph. 2:13)

Through the door opened up by Jesus into God's presence we are in a new dimension of reality. This is far greater than any psychic "altered consciousness" - it is truly a new reality.

We can now live in direct connection with the throne of heaven and the Presence of God.

In the days of the Temple only the High Priest was permitted into the Holy of Holies once a year, but now everyone who comes in sincerity can come through the blood of Jesus into God's presence. What a tremendous privilege!

"Having therefore, brethren, boldness to enter into the holy place by the blood of Jesus, by the way which He dedicated for us, a new and living way, through the veil, that is to say, his flesh; and having a great priest over the house of God; let us draw near with a true heart in fullness

of faith, having our hearts sprinkled from an evil conscience: and having our body washed with pure water." (Hebrews 10:19-22)

We have been brought near to Him and can now enter a life of intimacy with God. His love comes flooding into our hearts by the Holy Spirit and our spirits are joined to His. (Romans 5) We become spiritually aware of His love, presence and care. From this love comes a new kind of worship. The awareness of His love propels us to spend time with Him and to seek greater intimacy. Our relationship with our Father becomes the most important relationship in our lives.

"God is spirit, and those who worship must worship in spirit and in truth." (John 4:24) To worship Him means not only to honor Him with the highest possible esteem but also means to enter into spiritual intimacy with God. God is looking for worshippers rather than workers.

Worship is our response to God's presence, to who He is and to what He has done. Through it we enjoy a relationship of love that becomes the highest most significant and wonderful relationship in our lives. Our time with Him, honoring Him and being still before Him is the greatest and most significant part of our day. Today when people think of worship they often limit it to worship music (which can be a valuable aid to worship). However, none of the New Testament references to worship involves music. Worship is our loving personal response to God acknowledging Him and reciprocating His love and mercy.

Because the blood of Jesus brings us into a dimension of closeness to God we express this in our conscious worship. We also carry this love and adoration of Him with us wherever we go. We are continually in the glow of His presence and we are worshiping not only by our communication with Him but by the way we live our lives.

In the light of worship and adoration the prayer of asking is also altered. It is no longer a "Gimmie; Gimmie; Gimmie." type of prayer but "Thank You; thank You; Thank You" – receiving love, responding to love, and abiding in His love and presence.

"No longer do I call you servants, for the servant does not know what his master does. But I have called you friends, for all things that I have heard from My Father I have made known to you." (John 15:15)

We pray as friends and not as strangers. God wants to share His abundance with us but He values more our loving response and relationship with Him. Time with Him receiving, acknowledging and returning His love is the greatest kind of prayer and our great privilege and joy.

It is good to ask God for everything, but it is even better to love Him and be His intimate friend. The blessings we receive from Him are no longer the main focus - they are the natural outcome of our relationship. When He becomes the love of our lives we continue to ask. but the asking comes out of the relationship.

"Be not anxious therefore, saying, what shall we eat? or, What shall we drink? or, how shall we be clothed? For after all these things do the Gentiles seek; for your heavenly Father knows that you have need of all these things. But seek first his kingdom, and his righteousness; and all these things shall be added unto you." (Mt. 6:31-33)

Worship At The Throne Of Heaven

The realm of the unseen is much greater than the realm of the seen. Our natural senses cannot touch this realm but our spiritual senses do. There we receive and soak up the love of God and the life that issues from His throne. Our spirits are "seated" with Jesus in the throne room of heaven and are in the same realm where the angels and glorified saints worship God continually.

Isaiah, Ezekiel, Daniel, John and others were privileged to see into this realm at times. They saw the angels and cherubim and the four living creatures around the throne of God. After we are 'born again' and united with God in the spirit we too can enter the presence of God absorbing the love and joy of the kingdom. Here we experience

- the power and authority of the Lord
- the joy and strength of the Lord
- the mercy and compassion of the Lord
- and mind surpassing communication with His awesome presence.

John describes this scene of worship:

"At once I was in the Spirit, and lo, a throne stood in heaven, with one seated on the throne! And He who sat there appeared like jasper and carnelian, and round the throne was a rainbow that looked like an emerald. Round the throne were twenty-four thrones, and seated on the thrones were twenty-four elders, clad in white garments, with golden crowns upon their heads.

From the throne issue flashes of lightning, and voices and peals of thunder, and before the throne burn seven torches of fire, which are the seven spirits of God; and before the throne there is as it were a sea of glass, like crystal. And round the throne, on each side of the throne, are four living creatures, full of eyes in front and behind: the first living creature like a lion, the second living creature like an ox, the third living creature with the face of a man, and the fourth living creature like a flying eagle.

And the four living creatures, each of them with six wings, are full of eyes all round and within, and day and night they never cease to sing, "Holy, holy, holy, is the Lord God Almighty, who was and is and is to come!" And whenever the living creatures give glory and honor and thanks to him who is seated on the throne, who lives for ever and ever, the twenty-four elders fall down before him who is seated on the throne and worship him who lives for ever and ever; they cast their crowns before the throne, singing, "Worthy art thou, our Lord and God, to receive glory and honor and power, for thou didst create all things, and by thy will they existed and were created." (Revelation 4:2-11)

"Then He showed me the river of the water of life, bright as crystal, flowing from the throne of God and of the Lamb through the middle of the street of the city; also, on either side of the river, the tree of life with its twelve kinds of fruit, yielding its fruit each month; and the leaves of the tree were for the healing of the nations." (Rev. 22:1-2)

There is a river – not of water but of love, mercy, truth, joy and power that flows from the throne of Jesus, the triumphant Lamb, and from the throne of His Father and ours. The worshipers behold this realm in their spirits and as they do this river flows over them and through them into the world around them.

This is why Jesus in teaching us to pray placed the phrase *"hallowed be Thy name"* as the preface of prayer. In His presence we are filled with awe and we join in the *"Holy, Holy, Holy"* of the redeemed in heaven and on earth as we delight in the majesty and glory of God. Beholding His glory, we receive everything from His fullness. It the privilege of every believer to contact God in this realm – the realm of His GLORY. We can make our home in this realm and be sustained from this realm. It is this realm of the glory of God that is the source of all power and effectiveness in prayer.

Prayer In The Spirit

Such a realm of glory requires a language beyond our earthly language and this is why God has given us the prayer language, or gift of tongues.

Paul writes *"I will pray with the spirit, and I will pray with the understanding also: I will sing with the spirit, and I will sing with the understanding also."* (1 Cor. 14:15)

Communication with God, who is so vastly greater than our minds, requires that we do not limit our worship to intelligible words alone. It also requires a worship that reaches beyond the limits of our minds. We have a need to express the inexpressible, and communicate beyond words. This takes place when we take time to simply "be" with God in silent love, and when we pray in the spirit.

Through our prayer language we can pray beyond the limit of our minds, and communicate beyond the reach of our intelligible words. Through it we utter mysteries to God, and pour out to Him words which the Spirit supplies. *"For one who speaks in a tongue speaks not to men but to God; for no one understands him, but he utters mysteries in the Spirit."* (I Cor. 14:2)

"Likewise the Spirit helps us in our weakness; for we do not know how to pray as we ought, but the Spirit himself

intercedes for us with sighs too deep for words. And He who searches the hearts of men knows what is the mind of the Spirit, because the Spirit intercedes for the saints according to the will of God." (Romans 8:26-27)

The restoration of the use of tongues in recent generations is giving fresh energy to God's people around the world. Through it we can maintain constant contact with God even when our minds are occupied with practical matters.

"Be filled with the Spirit; speaking one to another in psalms and hymns and spiritual songs, singing and making melody with your heart to the Lord; giving thanks always for all things in the name of our Lord Jesus Christ to God, even the Father." (Ephesians 5:18-19)

"But you, beloved, building yourselves up by your most holy faith, praying in the Holy Spirit, keep yourselves in the love of God, eagerly awaiting the mercy of our Lord Jesus Christ to everlasting life." (Jude 20-21)

Prayer in the spirit strengthens us, keeps us in the realm of God's love and glory where the rivers of His life and love stream forth. What a privilege we have to enter the Throne Room to worship and adore Him and go beyond the limit of our natural minds and natural understanding!

"After these things I looked, and behold, a door was opened in Heaven. And the first voice, which I heard, was as it were of a trumpet talking with me, saying, Come up here, and I will show you what must occur after these things. And immediately I became in spirit. And behold, a throne was set in Heaven, and One sat upon the throne." (Revelation 4:1-2)

Chapter 3

The Cross- & The Blessing

The Atoning Sacrifice of Jesus has transformed prayer forever. We are no longer praying to force our will on God. We no longer pray as strangers begging for crumbs but as honored guests invited to a banquet with the wedding garment provided. We come to Him as heirs to receive our inheritance. God invites the outcasts of the world to come to this banquet, and gives them robes of His own making to qualify them to sit with Him at His table of blessing.

"But now in Christ Jesus you who were once afar off are made near by the blood of Christ." (Eph. 2:13)

"And He came and preached peace to you who were afar off, and to those who were near." (Eph. 2:17)

Sin came into the world through Adam's offence. With sin came death, poverty, sickness, guilt, condemnation and separation from God's blessings. Yet, as soon as this separation came, God promised to send someone to remove the division, guilt, and sickness and to restore the blessing. God made this promise first to Adam and then later to Abraham. (Genesis 3:15; Genesis 12:3)

Isaiah 53 records this promise in the greatest detail. There he predicted the coming of a Suffering Servant who would take on Himself our guilt and restore us to God's blessing. The fulfillment of this promise of redemption is the great theme of the Bible from Genesis to Revelation. Jesus' death and resurrection fulfilled this promise. The gospel is the announcement that indeed God in Jesus has borne the sins and guilt of the world. Furthermore, it is the invitation to all to come and receive the benefits of what God has provide in Jesus.

"Who has believed what we have heard? And to whom has the arm of the LORD been revealed?"

For he grew up before him like a young plant, and like a root out of dry ground; he had no form or comeliness that we should look at him, and no beauty that we should desire him.

He was despised and rejected by men; a man of sorrows, and acquainted with grief; and as one from whom men hide their faces he was despised, and we esteemed him not.

Surely he has borne our griefs and carried our sorrows; yet we esteemed him stricken, smitten by God, and afflicted.

But he was wounded for our transgressions, he was bruised for our iniquities; upon him was the chastisement that made us whole, and with his stripes we are healed.

All we like sheep have gone astray; we have turned every one to his own way; and the LORD has laid on him the iniquity of us all.

He was oppressed, and he was afflicted, yet he opened not his mouth; like a lamb that is led to the slaughter, and like a sheep that before its shearers is dumb, so he opened not his mouth.

By oppression and judgment he was taken away; and as for his generation, who considered that he was cut off out of the land of the living, stricken for the transgression of my people?

And they made his grave with the wicked and with a rich man in his death, although he had done no violence, and there was no deceit in his mouth.

Yet it was the will of the LORD to bruise him; he has put him to grief; when he makes himself an offering for sin, he shall see his offspring, he shall prolong his days; the will of the LORD shall prosper in his hand;

he shall see the fruit of the travail of his soul and be satisfied; by his knowledge shall the righteous one, my servant, make many to be accounted righteous; and he shall bear their iniquities." (Isaiah 53:1-11)

This prophecy is an exact description of the sufferings of Jesus and was written 600 years before they happened! He exactly fulfilled this prophecy in His suffering, death and resurrection.

God made elaborate and extravagant plans to restore us to fellowship and favor with Himself. Sin and the curse stood in the way, so God laid our guilt and sin on Jesus. He yearned for reconciliation with us so much that He interposed Jesus between our sins and guilt to reconcile us to Himself. As one friend said, *"God did not send Jesus primarily to die for our sins. He wanted to restore us to His care. Sin was in the way - so He sent Jesus to remove the sin that stood between us and His blessing."*

We see that on the cross Jesus took the *four great negative emotions*

- guilt
- grief
- sorrow and
- rejection.

These emotions are the source of 'the broken heart' from which most of our mental torments come. Jesus came to heal the brokenhearted by taking these curses on Himself.

"The Spirit of the Lord God is upon me for the Lord has anointed me to heal the broken hearted ... to give them beauty for ashes the oil do joy for mourning and the garment of praise for the spirit of heaviness." (Isaiah 60:10)

People everywhere are burdened with guilt, sorrow, pain and sickness. Jesus took all this on Himself. As we put our faith in Him we can release our guilt, sorrow, pain and sickness to Him. In this way, He can 'extract' these things from us. He then adds the Holy Spirit to us replacing our guilt with forgiveness, our pain with peace, our sorrow with joy, our sickness with life. Jesus removes the negatives by His cross and adds the positive through the Holy Spirit. He said, *"the thief comes to steal kill and destroy but I am come that they may have life and have it more abundantly."* (John 10:10) His work is to undo the devastation that has come upon us through the sin of the world, our own sin and the oppression of the devil.

"The reason the Son of God appeared was to destroy the works of the devil." (1 John 3:8) This includes every obstacle to our access in prayer.

The Blessing

Through His work on the cross Jesus redeemed us from the "curse of the law." *"Christ has redeemed us from the curse of the law having become a curse for us so that the blessings of Abraham might come upon us gentiles through faith that we might receive the promised Holy Spirit."* (Galatians 3:13)

In Deuteronomy Chapter *28 "the curse of the law"* is described as sickness, diseases, confusion and financial misery. Jesus took *"the curse of the law"* on Himself so that we can now be restored to God and blessed by Him as Abraham was. The Scriptures tell us that God blessed Abraham *"in all things"* and to be a blessing to others. (Genesis 24:1; & 12:3)

Jesus' death on the cross opens the way for all believers to receive the blessings of Abraham i.e. to be blessed in all things and to be a blessing to others. When we come to God based on faith in what Jesus has done, we receive not only forgiveness of sin but also the replacement of the curse of the law with the blessings of Abraham. That is good news for all the oppressed people of the world. The kingdom of God's mercy, care and blessing is available to all through faith in the gospel!

We are now living at *"the reverse side of the cross."* It has already happened - the sin has been atoned for, the veil in the temple has been rent, and the curse has been borne. The provision for restoration and blessing has already been made. It simply remains for us to receive.

Prayer works in partnership with the good news of what Jesus has done. Our boldness in prayer stands on the foundation of the Cross. The word announces what God has made available for us in Jesus. It remains for us simply to appropriate these blessings through faith. Prayer is the act by which we receive from God that which He offers. As the revelation of the good news of what God has made available to all men through Jesus reaches every nation, a revolution of love and mercy will cover the earth. Prayer will yet be recognized as the most important and practical activity that we can ever engage in.

Chapter 4

The Prayer Of Agreement

In the secular world business is transacted by means of contracts. Contracts are ratified by written agreements. These agreements are made of written words which become binding on the parties involved in the contract.

- Secular business is transacted by means of written words.
- Spiritual business is transacted by means of spoken words.

Thus, for example, in a marriage ceremony the couple seal their vow by the simple phrase "I do." This simple use of words changes their relationship from friendship to marriage.

God has given us the ability to transact business on earth and in heaven. With our spoken words of agreement we consent to or reject His will for our lives. If we release our words of consent to Him in prayer, we allow Him to become more involved in our lives to help, bless and direct us. This consent, released in words, authorizes Him to accomplish His benign and wonderful will in our lives.

God will not *impose* His will upon us. Instead He *offers us* His will and *invites us* to embrace it. This invitation is revealed in the promises of the scriptures We can plainly read what God makes available to us so that we know exactly what we can pray for. In faith we come into agreement with God's will and in prayer we vocalize this agreement and make it formal

"His divine power has given to us all things that pertain to life and godliness, ... through which He has given to us exceedingly great and precious promises, so that by these you might be partakers of the divine nature, having escaped the corruption that is in the world through lust." (2 Peter 1:3-4)

Two Kingdoms

There are two kingdoms in the unseen realm - the kingdom of darkness and the kingdom of light. The kingdom of Light is the kingdom of God where His will and rule prevail. The kingdom of darkness is opposed to God and His will. When we enter God's kingdom through the atoning sacrifice we are translated from the Kingdom of darkness to the kingdom of Light. Paul writes that God has *"delivered us out of the power of darkness, and translated us into the kingdom of the Son of his love."* (Colossians 1:13)

We are now in a new realm. The darkness that once oppressed us has lost its dominion over us and we are now in the light and blessing of God's love and rule.

The struggle is not completely over, however, because our minds need to be retrained to think in the light of our new situation. We have to put off old ways of thinking, speaking and acting and develop an attitude of hope and confidence that reflects the Kingdom we are now in.

"Put off your old nature which belongs to your former manner of life and is corrupt through deceitful lusts, and be renewed in the spirit of your minds, and put on the new nature, created after the likeness of God in true righteousness and holiness. Therefore, putting away falsehood, let every one speak the truth with his neighbor, for we are members one of another. Be angry but do not sin; do not let the sun go down on your anger, and give no opportunity to the devil." (Ephesians 4:22-27)

"Do not be conformed to this world but be transformed by the renewal of your mind, that you may prove what is the will of God, what is good and acceptable and perfect." (Romans 12:2)

Breaking With Darkness & Embracing His Light

"But you are a chosen race, a royal priesthood, a holy nation, God's own people, that you may declare the wonderful deeds of him who called you out of darkness into his marvelous light." (1 Peter 2:9)

To establish the rule of the kingdom of God in our minds we "cancel" agreement with all thoughts, attitudes and words spoken by us, to us or about us, that are contrary to the reality of God's kingdom, ways and word. Many believers are bombarded by negative and unwelcome thoughts and imaginations such as unclean thoughts, thoughts of despair and discouragement, paranoid thoughts etc. Such thoughts may have come to us through family and culture, through hurtful words or through painful life experiences. Not knowing any better we tend to agree with these thoughts and pronouncements. This agreement establishes those thoughts and develops within us attitudes of fear powerlessness and negativity.

Where we have consciously or unconsciously assented to ideas that are not in harmony with His will, we can now

- *break our agreement* with these thoughts and attitudes and
- *embrace the will of God.*

It is our responsibility to resist the powers of darkness and sin and not to permit them to reestablish their rule over us through lies that infect our thoughts and words.

"For sin shall not have dominion over you, for you are not under Law, but under grace." (Romans 6:14)

Jesus showed us how to do this when He was confronted by the Devil in the wilderness. (See Luke chapter 4) There He was bombarded by many strange and crazy thoughts, which came from Satan, ruler of the kingdom of darkness. Jesus, recognizing that these thoughts were not in

harmony with God's word and kingdom
- refused to come into agreement with them
- and commanded the spirit (Satan) behind these thoughts to leave Him.

In this way, unwise, negative and insane thoughts were unable to get any ground in His life. He refused to entertain thoughts that had their origin in the kingdom of darkness.

We can all *"overcome as He overcame."* (Revelation 3:21) The Holy Spirit empowers us to rule over our thoughts and words and to resist crazy thoughts and lies that have their origin in the Kingdom of darkness. Through Him we can *"take every thought captive."* *"We destroy arguments and every proud obstacle to the knowledge of God, and take every thought captive to obey Christ."* (2 Cor. 10:5) We too can refuse to come into agreement (and cancel any past agreement) with any thought not in harmony with God's word and God's kingdom. We can also command any spirit that has had access to us with these thoughts to leave us in Jesus' Name. To take every thought captive we simply:
- cancel agreement with every thought that is contrary to the benign will of God and
- command any spirit behind that thought to leave.

The first sign to accompany believers in

Jesus is the ability to expel demons. *"And these signs will accompany those who believe: in my name they will cast out demons; they will speak in new tongues; they will pick up serpents, and if they drink any deadly thing, it will not hurt them; they will lay their hands on the sick, and they will recover."* (Mark 16:17-18)

This does not mean that every believer is to go around casting demons from people - but that all believers have the power to expel the oppressing low level spirits that seek to cloud our minds with dark thoughts. We deal not only with unwelcome thoughts but also with the spirits that transmit these thoughts to us. Jesus has given us authority in this area on the basis of His triumph over the Kingdom of darkness. This authority over illegal spirits is not limited to specially gifted individuals but belongs to every believer in Jesus. Since Jesus has already defeated the devil and his demons, the believer's task is simply to "expel" and "resist." We have complete authority over any spirit with an assignment to oppress or harass us.

When we come into the kingdom of God we have the power to break our agreement with these attitudes and to take authority over any illegal spirit behind these thoughts to leave us.

Agreement & Keys Of The Kingdom

What we agree with will decide our destiny. When we agree with negative and oppressing thoughts we give consent and yield ground to the kingdom of darkness. On the other hand when we cancel agreement with such thoughts and embrace (through verbal agreement) the plan of God, we make way for the Kingdom of God to be established in our lives.

Agreement (released with our words) is the essence of prayer:

- We cancel agreement by consciously vocalizing our disagreement with and renouncing any attitude or false belief that has established itself in our lives.

- We enter into agreement with the blessings and realities of God's kingdom by consciously and deliberately vocalizing our agreement with them.

When Peter acknowledged Jesus as the Messiah, Jesus gave him the "keys of the kingdom," which is the power to bind and loose – to make and cancel agreements.

"I tell you, you are Peter, and on this rock I will build my church, and the powers of death shall not prevail against it. I will give you the keys of the kingdom of heaven, and whatever you bind on earth shall be bound in heaven, and whatever you loose on earth shall be loosed in heaven." (Matthew 16:18 - 19)

Later Jesus gave the same ability to bind and to loose to every disciple.

"Truly, I say to you, whatever you bind on earth

shall be bound in heaven, and whatever you loose on earth shall be loosed in heaven. Again I say to you, if two of you agree on earth about anything they ask, it will be done for them by my Father in heaven." (Matthew 18:18-19)

Jesus called this power to bind and to loose *"the keys of the kingdom."* He gave His disciples the amazing power to "bind on earth what is bound in heaven," i.e. to release heavens will on the earth. This is astonishing power. Our formal verbal agreement with God's plan and word actually releases heavens' will and blessings on the earth.

When millions of followers of Jesus begin to wake up to their priestly authority and exercise it we shall see a revolution of blessing on the earth. Prayer will no longer be seen as the refuge of the religious but as the tool of kings.

John writes that *God "has made us kings and priests to God."* (Revelation 1:6) There has been much talk about the *"priesthood of all believers"* but little demonstration of the power of an army of hundreds of millions coming into agreement with God and releasing His good will on the earth. God is looking for His followers to begin to exercise dominion on the earth through prayer and to advance His kingdom by the use of the keys of the kingdom. The *"priesthood of all believers"* is about to be harnessed like electric power as a practical force to transform the earth.

The prayer of agreement is an astonishing gift from God and is one of the great keys to advancing His kingdom on the earth – agreement, his word and others with the same renewed mind.

"Again I say to you, if two of you agree on earth about anything they ask, it will be done for them by my Father in heaven." (Mt. 18:19)

Chapter 5

The Three Dimensions Of Prayer

When we pray we pray in three dimensions:

- **Upwardly** to God the Father in Jesus' Name in accordance with John 16:26, Isaiah 45:11, Mark 11:24 etc.
- **Outwardly** in declaration and blessing pronouncing words of life into the situation we are praying for, in Jesus' Name, in accordance with God's will. (See Numbers 6:23-25, Mark 11:23 etc.
- **Downwardly** against all hindering spirits that stand in the way of these blessings, in Jesus' Name in accordance with Mark 11:23: Jas. 4:7 etc.

Upward Prayer

"In that day you will ask in my name; and I do not say to you that I shall pray the Father for you; for the Father himself loves you, because you have loved me and have believed that I came from the Father." (John 16:26-27)

- *"Thus says the LORD, the Holy One of Israel, and his Maker, Ask me of things to come concerning my sons, and concerning the work of my hands command ye me."* (Isaiah 45:11)

Upward prayer is made upward to God from earth to heaven. True prayer, as we have seen, is made to God - the God of the Bible and Father of Our Lord Jesus Christ.

As we approach God we approach Him through the blood of Jesus aware of His awesome power and might. We believe that we are speaking to Him, that He is listening to us, and that He will respond and act to bring the answers to our prayers.

Praying With Boldness

"Therefore, brethren, since we have confidence to enter the sanctuary by the blood of Jesus, by the new and living way which he opened for us through the curtain, that is, through his flesh. And since we have a great priest over the house of God, let us draw near with a true heart in full assurance of faith, with our hearts sprinkled clean from an evil conscience and our bodies washed with pure water." (Hebrews 10:19-22)

When we pray upward to God through Jesus we can pray in complete confidence that He is listening to us. The atoning sacrifice of Jesus gives us access to God the Father, to the throne room of heaven, the control room of the universe - God's office!

We pray:
- with a new access
- with a new revelation of God's will
- in the name of Jesus.

This is what gives the believers' prayer so much authority and why it is so radically different from any other kind of prayer, or from the prayer that is exercised in the religions of the world.

"And this is the confidence, which we have in him, that if we ask anything according to his will He hears us." (1 John 5:14)

We are not ignorant about what God's will is because, as we have seen, the Bible reveals it to us. Where the word of God makes it clear what God's will is - and it does on so many issues - we can be absolutely confident that God will act. *Upward prayer is based on God's promises* and the relationship we have with Him through Jesus the Messiah.

"If you abide in me, and my words abide in you, ask whatever you will, and it shall be done for you." (1 John 5:7)

Those who are saturated in the teaching of Jesus know God's will and can, therefore, pray in line with God's purposes. Once we know what God's will is, we are in a position of tremendous authority in our prayer. We can remove the curse and appropriate the blessings we spoke about in Chapter 3.

Commanding God!?

"Thus says the LORD, the Holy One of Israel, and his Maker, Ask me of things to come concerning my sons, and concerning the work of my hands command ye me." (Isaiah 45:11)[1]

Does God actually ask us to **command Him** i.e. to demand that He does certain things? At first this seems quite offensive to our religious sensibilities. After all, it is the Lord who commands us to obey Him. Yet He does ask us to command Him in one specific area – the area of praying His will. He wants us to command Him to do His will on the earth. The reason He asks us to command Him to do His work, is based on two principles that govern the earth:

1) The *free will*, which God has given us
2) The *dominion*, which God has given us

God could overwhelm us with His power but then He would be forcing His will on us. Because of the principle of free will, God has chosen not to bypass man in His rule of earth. He does not act without our prayer because then He would have to bypass our wills. He wants us *to recognize and choose His will*. He is waiting for His prayer partners to come into

---

[1] Some translators read "Do you command me?" instead of "Command ye me." They reverse the meaning of the original Hebrew and conceal the tremendous offer God makes to those who pray to Him.

agreement with Him. He has a sovereign plan to bring to pass but He can only bring it to pass with our cooperation.

Without God - we cannot
Without us - God will not

That is why when He wants something done He reveals His will to us and requires that we pray and act in line with His will.

God's Word shows us what He wants us to ask Him. "*Surely the Lord GOD does nothing, without revealing his secret to his servants the prophets.*" (Amos 3:7)

When we pray in line with the Word of God we are, therefore, praying the Will of God. We are then cooperating with God in bringing to pass His wonderful will for us and for the world.

Prayer is God's way of getting His will done on the earth without bypassing man's free will. God has ordained prayer as the conduit to release His will on the earth. It is through prayer that we can welcome, receive and embrace His will into the earth.

The dominion that Adam lost in the Garden Christ is restoring to His Bride. When we submit to His ways and His word, we can begin exercise through the Name of Jesus the dominion He destined us to have on the earth.

This is not an exercise of our independent will, but a cooperative dominion in union with Him to release His will upon the earth.

Prayer is like a light switch that allows the electricity to flow to light the bulb. The power plant has the power and the will to put light in the bulb but until the owner of the house turns the switch, the light cannot come on. Thus, prayer harmonizes the will of God and the will of man in a powerful and transforming accord.

Prayer does not change God's will but embraces and welcomes God's power to bring changes in our lives and in our world. When we "command God" we are not engaging our wills *against* Him but *with Him* to see His purposes established. We can say: *"I must insist. Lord. that you involve Yourself in this situation. and that Your will be done in this situation."* He looks for people who will lock their wills resolutely together with His.

This is why one of the greatest recorded prayers is the prayer of Mary in response to the message of the angel. The angel revealed God's will to bring the Messiah into the world through her. Her response: *"Be it done to me according to your word."* (Luke 1:38) released God's will into her life. Once God's word and will were revealed she could pray and command that His will be done. Without her assent the Messiah could not have come through her. Her "yes" to God's revealed will released His plan in the world. Through prayer she embraced God's plan and opened a highway for Him to perform His will. God waits for our prayers to release His will into our world.

PRAYER MOVES HEAVEN

The most amazing thing about prayer is that it moves heaven. *"Action on earth precedes action in heaven for earth governs heaven. … Here we see the principle of God's working, the secret of His action; whatever He wills to do, if man does not will, He will not do it. We cannot make God do what He does not want to do but we can hinder Him from doing what He does want to do."* (Watchman Nee "The Prayer Ministry of the Church" pages 9 & 10.)

This is why (as surprising as it sounds) God actually does indeed ask us to command Him, for prayer releases His hand to bring His purposes to pass.

Jesus also taught about demanding and commanding prayer. *"Whatever you ask in my name, I will do it, that the Father may be glorified in the Son; if you ask anything in my name, I will do it."* (John 14:13-14) When He says that we can ask the Father anything in His name - the idea is that we can make demands on God's mercy and God's promises on the ground of our covenant relationship with Him in the Name of Jesus. This asking is an authoritative and confident asking. It is not that we are imposing our will on God but opening up a channel through which God's redemptive and benign will can be released.

The Status Quo Is Not The Will Of God

Jesus asks us to pray that God's *"will be done on earth as it is in heaven."* The assumption here is that God's will is not yet being perfectly manifested on the earth. The heartbreak, sickness, famine, poverty, dissension, disharmony and strife that are on the earth are obviously not God's will and they are not God's doing. In the face of a fragmented and disharmonious world, He asks us to call down Hiss saving and healing will into our world:

- Hope where there is despair
- pardon where there is injury
- forgiveness where there is strife
- revelation where there is darkness
- love where there is indifference
- salvation where there is separation from Him and his will
- healing where there is sickness
- purpose where there is despair etc.

All real prayer is based on the realization that God's will for our lives and for the world around us is better than the way things are. The status quo is not the will of God.

Passive religion (such as is found among the Hindus and Moslems) teaches that there is nothing to be done in the face of life's difficulties except endure. Sadly, all too often this kind of passivity is found also among believers. Certainly we should know how to endure hardship and walk in patience and perseverance but we should also be contending continuously for the highest will and purpose of God to be established in our world and in our circumstances.

Where God's will is not being done, we can respond in patience, endurance and in compassion. This compassion should drive us to prayer that God's will would triumph in the circumstance and prevail. Through the word of God, we have a clear revelation of God's will and we can call on God with bold and confident prayer that His will be established in the situations we are praying about. Because we now have a revelation of what God's will is we need never be passive but work and pray for the status quo to change.

Where there is no resistance to and complete agreement with God's will, prayer can be made with utter confidence. For example, if believers in a church are all together in harmony for God to pour out the spirit of evangelism on the congregation, there will be a speedy answer to that prayer. However, if only some of the congregation is in agreement, there may be a division between those who want the spirit of evangelism to be released and those who do not. Thus because of opposition (or lack of openness to His will) God's hand can be hindered from sending His full blessing to the congregation. Where other wills are involved, blockages to God's will may hinder God's answer to prayer.

Usually the reason that prayer is not effective is because man's will has not come into agreement with God's will. The breakdown is not in God's will but in mans' will.

True intercessors cry out for God's will to be done in areas where it is obvious that it is not yet being done. We can change our lives and change the world by releasing God's will through asking, demanding and commanding prayer.

Outward Prayer

The second dimension of prayer is outward or ***declarative prayer***. Once we have prayed God's will we can now declare His will. We can speak forth the word of God that we have prayed. This kind of speaking forth is called "confession." We are to confess and profess forth what we believe God is doing. This is one of the most important mechanisms by which we release our faith.

Outward or horizontal prayer must reinforce vertical prayer to God. *"Without faith it is impossible to please God."* (Hebrews 11:6) Faith is released through confession and so declarative confession is a key ingredient in faith,

Jesus speaks about this *also "Truly, I say to you, whoever says to this mountain, 'Be taken up and cast into the sea,' and does not doubt in his heart, but believes that what he says will come to pass, it will be done for him. Therefore I tell you, whatever you ask in prayer, believe that you have received it, and it will be yours."* (Mark 11:23-24)

Jesus invites us to believe that **what we say** will come to pass. He encourages us not only to ask Him but also **to speak forth and declare confidently** what God's will is and believe that it will come to pass. The assumption here, of course, is that the thing we declare is in line with the will of God and the word of God.

We prophetically confess God's will into situations. We can declare forth that certain events that we have prayed for with confidence will happen in accordance with God's will.

Often there is a breakdown in prayer when people pray one thing upwardly to God, then outwardly say things contrary to what they have just prayed. Someone may pray for a certain blessing to come their way and then say such things as *"I know nothing will happen;" "I never get healed by God"* etc. The negative confession has totally negated the vertical prayer to God and indicates that they have prayed without faith.

Once vertical prayer has been made in line with God's will, we should boldly profess that what we have prayed will come to pass. We should remain in an attitude of confident receptivity until we see our prayers answered.

The declaration of the believer is actually part of God's instrumentality in bringing to pass His word. God delegates this extraordinary ability to believers.

The prophets modeled this kind of prayer. For example when the patriarchs blessed their children by professing words of blessing over them, those words spoken over their sons came to pass. Elijah called down fire on the altar on Mount Carmel. Ezekiel commanded the Spirit to bring life into the far off generations of Israelis. (Ezekiel 37)

The 23rd Psalm – A Prayer Of Confession

The 23rd is one of the most beloved prayers throughout the world:

- The LORD is my Shepherd;
- I shall not want.
- He makes me to lie down in green pastures;
- He leads me beside the still waters.

- He restores my soul; He leads me in paths of righteousness for His name's sake.
- Yea, though I walk through the valley of the shadow of death, I will fear no evil; for You are with me;
- Your rod and Your staff, they comfort me.
- You prepare a table for me in the presence of my enemies;
- You anoint my head with oil; my cup runs over.
- Surely goodness and mercy shall follow me all the days of my life;
- And I shall dwell in the house of the LORD forever. (Psalm 23:1-6)

This remarkable prayer contains no vertical, upward prayer, whatever! It is all horizontal, declarative prayer and yet it is universally regarded as one of the most perfect prayers.

Declarative prayer was understood in ancient days and we need to reclaim today. *"You also decree a thing, and it shall be established unto thee; and light shall shine upon thy ways."* (Job 22:28)

The prayer of confession or profession - declarative prayer is also a form of blessing. To bless is not just to make a nice wish for someone. It is to direct God's good will towards that person.

A blessing send forth by a righteous man will come to pass unless there are some obstructions in the receiver to block the blessing.

Peter writes that we are *"a chosen race, a royal priesthood, a holy nation, God's own people, that you may declare the wonderful deeds of him who called you out of darkness into his marvelous light."* (1 Peter 2:9) As priests of the Most High God interceding according to His revealed will, we too can declare the deeds of God into our world.

This power to bless was given to the Old Testament Priests in a special way. And so the High Priest after, atonement was made for sin, would pronounce the blessing over the congregation.

"Say to Aaron and his sons, Thus you shall bless the people of Israel: you shall say to them:
- *The Lord bless you and keep you;*
- *The Lord make his face to shine upon you, and be gracious to you;*
- *The Lord lift up his countenance upon you, and*
- *give you peace.*

So shall they put my name upon the people of Israel, and I will bless them." (Numbers 6:23-27)

Atonement takes care of the curse and opens the way for the priest to bless. Only that which is covered by the blood of atonement can be blessed. Acting in the Name of Jesus we too can speak forth God's word, God's will and God's blessings into the situations of lives.

As we recover and reclaim *"the priesthood of all believers,"* we are also rediscovering the power to bless. The priesthood of all believers does not mean that the priesthood is abolished but that the anointing, authority and responsibility of priesthood is offered to all believers. The true priesthood is about to be reclaimed, regained and exercised in a massive way by the sincere believers of this generation.

Downward Prayer

In every sphere of prayer we pray upwardly to God, outwardly in blessing and confession, and downwardly against hindering spirits on the earth blocking these prayers and blessings.

Downward prayer is the commanding words we direct to hindering and stealing spirits that seek to block the inflow of God's will and God's kingdom. It is not necessary to do this every time we pray but occasionally we do need to take authority over any force or illegal spirit trying to hinder our prayer.

Since prayer advances God's kingdom in the world, it also usurps the oppressive power of the kingdom of darkness. Jesus by His atonement has destroyed the authority of the evil one. Though the devil and His demons have lost their authority, they are still present to oppose God's kingdom. It is our responsibility through prayer and obedience to see that God's kingdom advance against the defeated but not fully displaced powers of darkness.

"Behold, I have given you authority to tread upon serpents and scorpions, and over all the power of the enemy; and nothing shall hurt you. Nevertheless do not rejoice in this, that the spirits are subject to you; but rejoice that your names are written in heaven." (Luke 10:19-20)

God has given great authority to redeemed believers. With this authority comes great responsibility. In submission to God we have the responsibility to rule over our own lives and over our areas of responsibility. This authority sometimes requires that we resist spiritual entities (evil spirits and demons) that oppose the advance of God's kingdom in our lives and areas of special responsibility.

Some believers are uncomfortable with this kind of prayer because it has not been traditionally taught in the churches. (Tradition has robbed us of so much.)

Jesus told His disciples that one of the marks of His followers is that they expel hindering and harassing demons. *"And these signs will accompany those who believe: in my name they will cast out demons;* [1] *they will speak in new tongues; they will pick up serpents, and if they drink any deadly thing, it will not hurt them; they will lay their hands on the sick, and they will recover. So then the Lord Jesus, after he had spoken to them, was taken up into heaven, and sat down at the right hand of God. And they went forth and preached everywhere, while the Lord worked with them and confirmed the message by the signs that attended it. Amen."* (Mk. 16:16 - 20)

The first sign that accompanies the believer is   exercise of authority over demons. This does not mean that believers have to fight or defeat the devil or any other demon. They are already defeated by the victory of Jesus on the Cross. As we have seen earlier, we simply have to expel them from our thoughts and from our lives and resist their operations and maneuvers against us and against our concerns.

Some believers ignore demons and some give them excessive attention. Those who ignore them have an incomplete prayer life and because of passivity can be hindered by illegal spirits. Those who pay too much attention to them lose sight of the victory of Jesus.

The believer stands on the ground of Jesus' victory knowing that every hindering spirit is illegal and can be expelled with a word of command.

Downward prayer is a prayer of command directed towards every hindering spirit that stands in the way of the advance of God's blessing into the areas we are praying about. We simply pray in the name of Jesus a prayer of command, commanding every spirit of accusation, intimidation, fear, infirmity strife, and confusion hindrance etc. from acting in the situation.

Many think that taking authority over evil spirits calls for a high level of spirituality. This is one of the ways tradition can rob believers of their authority. Jesus thanked the Father that He had revealed these things not to the wise and learned but to mere children.

"At that time Jesus declared, "I thank thee, Father, Lord of heaven and earth, that thou hast hidden these things from the wise and understanding and revealed them to babes." (Mt. 11:25)

Jesus made authority over evil spirits the privilege of every believer. It is not reserved for the most educated but it is the heritage of the simplest believer.

A word of caution is appropriate here however. We are not required to take authority over every spirit out there. We take authority over spirits that we discern are hindering the plans of God in our own lives and area of dominion or in the lives of those we are praying for or ministering to. Man's dominion is on the earth. Jesus has authority over all spirits on heaven and on earth. We should exercise authority only over those spirits that are working on the earth against God's kingdom in the area of our direct responsibility.

"The heavens are the Lord's heavens, but the earth he has given to the sons of men." (Psalm 115:16)

Life Changing, World Changing Prayer

While God's dominion is over the heavens and the earth, man's dominion is confined to the earth. We are not required to exercise dominion over the spirits in the heavenlies such as "the rulers of the darkness of this present age" and the *"hosts of wickedness in the heavenly places."* (Ephesians 6:12) We should leave them to the Lord to handle and simply say: *"The Lord rebuke you."* (Jude 1:9) In dealing with spirits operating on the earth against our minds and bodies, we can take authority directly over them.

Chapter 6

The Seven Spheres Of Prayer

There are seven major spheres in which our priestly ministry of prayer can be exercised. Through the exercise of the true ministry of prayer – the ministry every believer - we the community of believers (the church) can change the destiny of our lives and of our nations.

The Seven Spheres Of Prayer

The seven spheres in which we have authority and responsibility to pray are:
1. Our Selves (Lk. 17.3, 1 Chr. 4.10; 1 Cor. 14.4)
2. Our Family (Eph. 3.15)
3. Our Church (Eph. 6.18,19)
4. Our City (1 Tm 2:2; Jer. 29:7)
5. Our Nation (1 Tm 2:2)
6. The Nation of Israel (Gn. 12:3; Ps. 122: 3)
7. The Nations (1 Tim. 2.2; Mt. 6:9-13)

When we pray in the three dimensions (UPWARD, OUTWARD and DOWNWARD) over these major spheres, our prayers will be immensely effective. We can pray for God's purposes in each of these spheres to come to pass. We pray "Your Kingdom come, Your will be done" in each of these areas of concern.

Firstly, we enter into His "office" - the throne room of heaven - boldly through the blood of Jesus with thanksgiving and confidence and make our request to Him as clearly as we can articulate them.

Secondly, we speak forth and confess that God is fulfilling these prayers.

Thirdly, we take authority over any spirit that would hinder the answer to these prayers.

1. Praying For Ourselves

Our first responsibility is to pray for ourselves because we are no good to others until we have the kingdom of God operating in our own lives. As Jesus said: *"How can you say to your brother, 'Let me take the speck out of your eye,' when there is the log in your own eye? You hypocrite, first take the log out of your own eye, and then you will see clearly to take the speck out of your brother's eye."* (Mt. 7:4-5)

"Take heed to yourself and to the doctrine; continue in them, for doing this you shall both save yourself and those who hear you." (1 Tim 4:16)

When we pray for ourselves we can pray that:

Life Changing, World Changing Prayer

- we will be filled with the Spirit of God, and the fruit of the Spirit (Gal 5.22)
- with wisdom, love and compassion and empowered to live a life pleasing to the Lord bearing fruit in every good work, and increasing in the knowledge and love of God. (Col. 1:10)
- We pray God's blessing on our spirit, soul, and body and that we will prosper and be in health even as our souls prosper (3 John 1)
- that He will keep us blameless in each of these realms (1 Thess. 5:24)
- that He will not only bless us more and more but also make us a greater blessing to others. (Genesis 12:3)
- We pray that the blessings of Abraham (who was blessed in all things) and which Jesus purchased for us will be upon us. (Gen. 24:1; Gal. 3:13-14)
- We pray that we will be anointed to be bold witness of the resurrection and do the works of a disciple. Etc. etc. (Acts 1:8; Jn. 14:12)
- We pray that we will be strengthened in our inner man . (Ephesians 3:16)
- We pray that we may fulfill the purpose He has for us on the earth and do the works He has created us for. (Ephesians 2:10)
- We pray that we will be filled with revelation and knowledge of His will; (Ephesians 1:16)
- That we will be empowered to love Him and our fellow man as He has loved us;

- That He will direct our paths and reveal Himself to us (Pv. 3:5; John 14:21) etc.

Then we speak forth that God is answering these prayers and releasing the blessing we have been praying for.

We take authority over any spirit hindering the blessings we have called down on our selves and loose (untie) ourselves from any entanglement with any attitudes, fears, imaginations and spirits that keep us from our destiny.

One can only imagine the impact on the world if every believer, and every young person in particular, prayed in this manner for themselves.

2. Praying For Our Families

The second sphere of prayer is for our families because we have special responsibly for them. For them we pray the same kind of prayers that we might make for ourselves:

- that they may have a revelation of God's mysteries and will (Ephesians 1:16)
- serve the Lord by living lives fully pleasing to Him. (Col. 1:9-10)
- We pray that they may be strong in spirit (Ephesians 3:14)
- blessed in all things (Genesis 24.1)

- kept blameless in spirit, soul and body (1 Thess. 5:23-24).
- We pray that each member of the family will fulfill their destiny in Christ (Eph. 2:10)
- know, love and serve the Lord (Mt. 22:37)
- be protected from the evil one (Jn. 17:15) etc. etc.

Then we speak forth that God is answering these prayers and the blessing we have been praying.

Finally, we take authority over any spirit hindering the blessings we have been calling down on our families and we loose (untie) them from any entanglement with thoughts attitudes, influences and spirits that might keep them from their destiny.

3. Praying For Our Church

The New Testament is packed with the prayers of the believing community the church.

The church exists through prayer, exercises its ministry through prayer; and develops through prayer. Jesus not only taught the church to pray and gave it authority in prayer, He also made the community of believers the special object of His prayer. *"I pray for them: I pray not for the world, but for those whom You have given me; for they are Yours; ... I pray not that you should take them from the world, but that you should keep them from the evil one. They are not of the world even as I am not of the world. Sanctify them in the truth: thy word is truth."* (John 17:9; 15-17)

If Jesus made the community of believers the special object of His prayer, we should also. The early church constantly prayed for itself and its mission. Prayer for the church and its mission is clearly a priority for every believer. Here, as in all cases of prayer, we pray best when we pray in line with the scriptures - the revealed will of God.

When we pray for the church we pray that it will be:

- effective in the world without being compromised by it; (Jn. 17:15)
- filled with boldness to fulfill its commission even in the face of opposition, (Acts 4:29)
- filled with love for God love for another and love for the lost; (John 13:34; Mt. 22:37)
- filled with a spirit of revelation, (Ephesians 1:16)
- faithful to the word of God, (2 Tm. 4.12)
- free from hindering tradition, (Mark 7:7)
- holy and blameless, (Eph. 1:4; Col. 1:22)
- generous to the poor (Gal. 2:10)
- abounding in the work of the Lord, (1 Cor. 15:58)
- obeying the Great Commission. (Mt 26:18; Lk. 10:2)
- directed by the Spirit (Rm. 8:14)

Life Changing, World Changing Prayer

- that God will extend His hand to heal and that signs and wonders will be demonstrated through the Name of Jesus (Acts 4:30)
- that it lacks for no good gift (1 Cor. 1:7)
- that it becomes a powerhouse of evangelism, hope and ministry in the area (Mt. 5:14)
- That the Lord will add to it those who are being saved. (Acts 5:14; 16;15)
- We pray for the leaders of the church that they will live lives worthy of their calling and accurately teach the word of God in an anointed, fruitful, joyful manner and in a spirit of love. (Phil 1:27)

In addition we can then pray for the specific needs and projects of our local church and for its leaders, people and those who receive its ministry.

We then confess that the blessings we are praying for are coming to pass and declare them forth.

We take authority over spirits working on the believers to keep them from their destiny. We especially take authority over spirits of strife and accusation working to destroy the unity of the church and its power to pray "in one accord."

This kind of prayer is even more effective when the entire local church in an area comes together to pray for its common mission.

4 & 5 Praying For Our Nation & City

"But seek the welfare of the city where I have sent you into exile, and pray to the LORD on its behalf, for in its welfare you will find your welfare." (Jer. 29:7)

"If My people, who are called by My name, shall humble themselves and pray, and seek My face, and turn from their wicked ways, then I will hear from Heaven and will forgive their sin and will heal their land." (2 Chronicles 7:14)

These scriptures are self-explanatory. We are urged to pray for the welfare and blessing of the city in which we live.

For our **nation** and **city** we pray:

• for all leaders of our city and nation
• the church in our city and nation
• the lost in our cities and nations
• for the word of God to be effectively proclaimed in our city and nation
• for the workers to go with the good news into every area of our city and nation places
• for peace in the city and nation,
• for the kingdom of God to impact every aspect of life in our city and nation including the economy, the education system, the legal system and officers of the law
• that God will raise up effective ministries to reach the lost, the youth and drug addicts etc.

We confess that the blessings we are praying for are coming to pass, and declare them forth.

"The earth is the Lord's, and the fullness of it; the world, and those who dwell in it." (Psalm 24:1)

Since the earth belongs to God, we can declare that our city and nation belong Him. We can cancel any false dedication of our city and nation to any other spirit and dedicate them back to God who owns them. We declare that Jesus is Lord.

We take authority only over spirits working on the earth hindering the answer to these prayers and hindering the advance of the gospel in our city and nation.

"First of all, then, I urge that supplications, prayers, intercessions, and thanksgivings be made for all men, for kings and all who are in high positions, that we may lead a quiet and peaceable life, godly and respectful in every way. This is good, and it is acceptable in the sight of God our Savior, who desires all men to be saved and to come to the knowledge of the truth." (1 Tim. 2:2)

Even though Paul lived under the tyrannical rule of the Roman Empire, he understood that it is an essential part of Christian ministry to pray for those in authority. Certainly we do not always agree with the government of our city and nation but we are always obliged to pray for them.

This prayer ministry of the church was functioning for more than fifteen hundred years before modern democracy. There is, undoubtedly, more power in prayer to influence the direction of our nation than in our vote - which is also our duty.

Prayer for our city and nation can be a part of each believer's personal prayer. This kind of prayer is even more powerful when large gatherings of believers come together to invoke God's kingdom and blessing on their kingdom and nation.

6. Pray For The Nations & The Harvest Fields

"I will bless those who bless you and I will curse those who cures you and in you all the families of the earth shall be blessed" (Gen 12:3)

"All the ends of the world shall remember and turn unto the LORD: and all the families of the nations shall worship before You." (Ps 22:27)

"Ask of me, and I shall give You the nations for your inheritance, and the uttermost parts of the earth for your possession." (Ps 2:8)

"Therefore he said to them, The harvest truly is great, but the laborers are few: pray therefore the Lord of the harvest, that he would send forth laborers into his harvest." (Luke 10:2)

Life Changing, World Changing Prayer

The purpose of God is clearly to bless all nations. He wants to bring them together in His love through Messiah Jesus. God promised Abraham to use His seed to bless all nations. (Genesis 12:3) Christians because of nationalistic loyalty sometimes lose sight of this great reality.

David asked for the nations. (Psalm 2:8) We, too, can pray that the nations will come under His blessing through the reconciliation that He has provided in Jesus. Jesus asked us to pray that His kingdom may come on all the earth and commanded us to go to the ends of the earth with the gospel.

The promise given to Abraham was that in him all the families of the earth (nations) would be blessed. The plan of God is that His redemptive blessings will reach the whole earth. So like Abraham, David and the apostles we should pray for the nations.

"First of all, then, I urge that supplications, prayers, intercessions, and thanksgivings be made for all men, for kings and all who are in high positions, that we may lead a quiet and peaceable life, godly and respectful in every way. This is good, and it is acceptable in the sight of God our Savior, who desires all men to be saved and to come to the knowledge of the truth." (1 Tim 2:1-4)

We pray for each nation:

- that it will hear the gospel of reconciliation, mercy and blessings (2 Cor. 5:17-21)

- that it will receive outpourings of the Holy Spirit (Joel 2:28-32)
- that God will send His workers and His word to that nation. (Here we pray that God will raise up indigenous workers for the gospel in that nation and send to them men and women who are truly appointed by Him. (Luke 10:2)
- that the kingdom of God will advance with all truth love and power in that nation (Mt. 6:10)
- that God will direct and shape the government in a way that best fits the advancement of the gospel and that, where necessary, He will change governments to favor the advance of the gospel and Kingdom of God. (1 Tim 2:1-4)

Then we speak forth and declare that God's will is being done in each nation we pray for.

In praying for the nations we are especially aware of the millions of believers who live in countries where the gospel is outlawed. It is estimated that about 160,000 are martyred each year for their faith. Christianity is the most persecuted religion in the world today and violence against Christians in increasing. We cannot be lulled by false teachings that Christians do not face tribulation. According to Zenit news agency some 200 million Christians suffer harsh repercussions because of their religion. A report presented in March 2013 to the *United Nations* in Geneva by the *WEF*, a global network of 160 million Evangelical Christians, also estimated that over 200 million Christians in at least 60 countries are denied fundamental human rights solely because of their faith.

The persecuted church and the families of those suffering for their faith must have a special place in our prayer. We pray that they will be strengthened and comforted through the Holy Spirit and that their obedience in the face of persecution will cause strongholds of opposition to the Kingdom of God to fall over the world.

"Remember the prisoners as if chained with them—those who are mistreated—since you yourselves are in the body also." (Hebrews 13:3)

7. Prayer For The Nation Of Israel

From all the nations, God has singled out one nation to have a special destiny. This is not because He loves them more than any other nation but because they have a special role to play in His plan for world redemption. Because of this calling we have a particular obligation to bless and pray for the nation of Israel.

Jerusalem is the only city that all believers are specifically asked to pray for. She who is the special object of God's call is also the special object of the destroyer and, therefore, uniquely in need of our prayers.

"Pray for the peace of Jerusalem: They shall prosper that love thee." (Psalm 122:6)

The ultimate triumph of the kingdom will be when Jesus the Messiah of the whole world takes His place as King of Israel and of the nations.

"Thus says the LORD of hosts: I was zealous for Zion with great zeal, and with great fervor I was zealous for her. Thus says the LORD: I will to Zion, and will dwell in the midst of Jerusalem: and Jerusalem shall be called a city of truth, and the mountain of the LORD of hosts, the holy mountain." (Zechariah 8:1-3)

When we pray for the Israel and for Jerusalem, we are really praying for the triumph of God's plan for world redemption. Sadly, Christianity for most of its history forgot to pray for the Jewish people and for Israel. Instead, it came into agreement with the spirit of anti-Semitism working through the ages to block God's purposes for Israel and for world redemption. However, this has begun to change as we approach the end of the age and as the truth of the Bible is being more accurately preached.

Blessing and praying for Israel is a divine mandate with a direct reward. *"And I will bless those that bless you and curse the one who curses you. And in you shall all families of the earth be blessed."* (Genesis 12:3)

For Israel we pray:

- that God will bless them in every way (Gen. 24:1)
- keep them safe in their land (Ps 121:3-4)
- that He will fulfill the promises of the prophets and bring them back from all the nations where they have been scattered. (Eze. 34:13; 37:12; Isa. 11:11-12)
- that He will sprinkle clean water on them, save them, sanctify them and pour out His Spirit upon them (Eze. 36:25; Jer. 31:33)
- that they might know their Messiah and discover the peace and power of the kingdom of God. (Zech. 12:10)
- that their leaders be wise, alert, guided by the Lord and surrendered to His will
- that the church be awakened to stand in love and solidarity with God's purposes and plans for the Israeli people and help them (Rom 11:25)
- that the indigenous believers in Israel may become a powerful force in the nation (Rom 11:23)
- that the Lord will protect and deliver Israel from its enemies (Ps. 122)
- that He pour clean water on them and cleanse them from their sins (Ezek. 37:23)
- liberate them from unbelief and traditions, which hinder them from recognizing the Messiah and entering the Kingdom of God (Romans 11:25)

- that God will fulfill all His plans for them to make them a blessing on the earth.

We then declare and speak forth that what we have prayed is coming forth. We declare that God's plan for Israel will be gloriously fulfilled.

We take authority over spirits of unbelief and religion that hinder their return to the land and their response to the gospel. We also take authority over the spirit of anti-Semitism (especially operating in Islam) to hinder the Lord's purposes for His land, His people and His kingdom.

Appendix 1

The Limits Of Prayer.

We have explored some of the dimensions and spheres of prayer. We see that prayer is the most important force in the universe for it marries the will of God and the will of man in a dynamic harmony that releases His will on the earth. As modern man has learned to harness the laws of electricity, electronics and aerodynamics, we have inadequately learned to harness the mighty power of prayer for practical good on the earth.

Yet there are some boundaries and limits of prayer. Though prayer is perhaps the greatest thing we can do on earth it is not the only thing we can do on the earth.

Some people work without prayer and others pray without work. Both prayer and work are necessary. Prayer is no substitute for the things that only work can do. We can pray for the energy to do our work, direction for our work, success and blessing in our work but prayer will never be a substitute for work. The best prayers are the best workers.

The great commission of the church to go to the ends of the earth with the good news of what God has accomplished in Jesus, cannot be accomplished by prayer alone. We pray for laborers to go into the harvest. And for all men to hear the good news. The prayer is no substitute for the actual labor involved in disseminating the good news.

Another limit on prayer is the time plan of God's redemptive plan. There are some aspects of God's plan that will not be accomplished until the Lord's return. The will of God is perfect but we do not see it perfectly manifested in our lives or on the earth at this present time. The forces that block His will are defeated but will not be removed from the earth and will remain until Jesus returns. Jesus warned us that the world will remain a dangerous place with wars, rumors of war, injustice, famines earthquakes and weather problems until the He returns. (Mt. 24:5-14)

Though we pray and labor for as much of God's kingdom to prevail on the earth, until the Lord returns, we know that much evil will remain with us until the Devil and his agents are driven from the planet. We will live our lives against the background of a suffering world, and compassionately work to alleviate that suffering.

Those who believe in Jesus already live in Our Father's kingdom, but the full triumph of His kingdom will not be manifested in the earth until the Lord returns and removes the devil (who has deceived all nations) from the earth.

So while we pray for the full triumph of the kingdom on earth and in our personal lives, we realize that God's blessings do not give us immunity from life's problems. Even the most powerful believer and prayer warrior will experience tribulation, suffering, hardship, persecution and labor until the Lord's return.

However, with prayer we can receive grace to handle even the most difficult situations with joy. The redemptive power of God turns the most difficult situations into a blessing when we pray. *"And we know that all things work together for good to those who love God, to those who are called according to His purpose. ...Truly He who did not spare His own Son, but delivered Him up for us all, how shall He not with Him also freely give us all things? Who shall separate us from the love of Christ? Shall tribulation, or distress, or persecution, or famine, or nakedness, or peril, or sword? As it is written, "For Your sake we are killed all the day long. We are counted as sheep of slaughter." But in all these things we more than conquer through Him who loved us. For I am persuaded that neither death, nor life, nor angels, nor principalities, nor powers, nor things present, nor things to come, nor height, nor depth, nor any other creature, shall be able to separate us from the love of God which is in Christ Jesus our Lord."* (Romans 8:28, 32, 35-39)

Appendix 2

The Great Prayer Promises

"In that day you will ask in my name; and I do not say to you that I shall pray the Father for you; for the Father himself loves you, because you have loved me and have believed that I came from the Father." (John 16:26-27)

"Whatever you ask in my name, I will do it, that the Father may be glorified in the Son; if you ask anything in my name, I will do it." (Jn. 14:13-14)

"In that day you will ask nothing of me. Truly, truly, I say to you, if you ask anything of the Father, He will give it to you in my name. Hitherto you have asked nothing in my name; ask, and you will receive, that your joy may be full." (John 16:23-24)

"Thus says the LORD, the Holy One of Israel, and His Maker, Ask me of things to come concerning my sons, and concerning the work of my hands command ye me" (Isaiah 45:11)

"And this is the confidence, which we have in him,

that if we ask anything according to His will He hears us. And if we know that He hears us whatever we ask, we know that we have the petitions we have asked of Him." (1 John 5:14 -15)

"If you abide in me, and my words abide in you, ask whatever you will, and it shall be done for you." (1 John 5:7)

"Truly, I say to you, whoever says to this mountain, 'Be taken up and cast into the sea,' and does not doubt in his heart, but believes that what he says will come to pass, it will be done for him. Therefore I tell you, whatever you ask in prayer, believe that you have received it, and it will be yours. And whenever you stand praying, forgive, if you have anything against any one; so that your Father also who is in heaven may forgive you your trespasses." (Mark 11:23-26)

"You desire and do not have; so you kill. And you covet and cannot obtain; so you fight and wage war. You do not have, because you do not ask. You ask and do not receive, because you ask wrongly, to spend it on your passions. Unfaithful creatures! Do you not know that friendship with the world is enmity with God? Therefore whoever wishes to be a friend of the world makes himself an enemy of God." (James 4:2-4)

"Whatever you ask in my name, I will do it, that the Father may be glorified in the Son; if you ask anything in my name, I will do it. (John 14:13-14)

APPENDIX 3

The Apostolic Prayers & The Prayers Of Jesus

The prayers of Jesus and the prayers of the apostles are model prayers for believers of all times.
We know we are praying at the living center of God's will when we pray these prayers deliberately and intelligently.

The recorded prayers of Jesus are "The Lord's Prayer " and Jesus' "High Priestly Prayer."
*   Matthew 6:9-13
*   John 17:20-26

The apostolic prayers recorded in the scriptures are found in the following references:

1.   Acts 4: 24-31
2.   Romans 10:1
3.   Romans 15:5-7
4.   Romans 15:13
5.   1 Corinthians 1:4-8
6.   Ephesians 1:17-19

Prayers Of Jesus

Matthew 6:9-13

"Therefore pray in this way: Our Father, who are in Heaven, Hallowed be Your name. Your kingdom come, Your will be done, on earth as it is in Heaven. Give us this day our daily bread; and forgive us our debts as we also forgive our debtors. And lead us not into temptation, but deliver us from the evil. For Yours are the kingdom, and the power, and the glory, forever. Amen." (Matthew 6:9-13)

John 17:20-26

"And I do not pray for these alone, but for those also who shall believe on Me through their word, that they all may be one, as You, Father, are in Me, and I in You, that they also may be one in Us, so that the world may believe that You have sent Me And I have given them the glory which You have given Me, that they may be one, even as We are one, I in them, and You in Me, that they may be made perfect in one; and that the world may know that You have sent Me and have loved them as You have loved Me.

Father, I desire that those whom You have given Me, that they may be with Me where I am, that they may behold My glory which You have given Me, for You have loved Me before the foundation of the world. O righteous Father, indeed the world has not known You; but I have known You, and these have known that You have sent me.

And I made known to them Your name, and will make it known, so that the love with which You have loved Me may be in them, and I in them." (John 17:20-26)

Prayers Of The Apostles

Acts 4:24-31

"And now, Lord, behold their threatenings, and grant to Your servants that with all boldness they may speak Your Word, by stretching forth of Your hand for healing, and miracles, and wonders may be done by the name of Your holy child Jesus. And when they had prayed, the place where they were assembled was shaken. And they were all filled with the Holy Spirit, and they spoke the Word of God with boldness." (Acts 4:24-31)

Romans 10:1

"Brothers, truly my heart's desire and prayer to God for Israel is for it to be saved." (Romans 10:1)

Romans 15:5-7

"And may the God of patience and consolation grant you to be like minded toward one another according to Christ Jesus, so that with one mind and one mouth you may glorify God, even the Father of our Lord Jesus Christ. Therefore receive one another as Christ also received us, to

the glory of God." (Romans 15:5-7)

Romans 15:13

"And may the God of hope fill you with all joy and peace in believing, that you may abound in hope through the power of the Holy Spirit." (Romans 15:13)

1 Corinthians 1:4-8

"I thank my God always on your behalf for the grace of God given you in Jesus Christ, that in everything you are enriched by Him, in all speech and in all knowledge; even as the testimony of Christ was confirmed in you; so that you come behind in no gift, waiting for the revelation of our Lord Jesus Christ. He shall also confirm you to the end, that you may be blameless in the day of our Lord Jesus Christ."
(1 Corinthians 1:4-8)

Ephesians 1:16-20

"I do not cease giving thanks for you, making mention of you in my prayers, that the God of our Lord Jesus Christ, the Father of glory, may give to you the spirit of wisdom and revelation in the knowledge of Him, the eyes of your understanding being enlightened, that you may know what is the hope of His calling, and what is the riches of the glory of His inheritance in the saints, and what is the surpassing greatness of His power toward us, the ones believing according to the working of His mighty strength which He worked in Christ in raising Him from the dead, and He seated Him at His right hand in the heavenlies." (Ephesians 1:16-20)

Ephesians 3:14-19

"For this cause I bow my knees to the Father of our Lord Jesus Christ, of whom the whole family in Heaven and earth is named, that He would grant you, according to the riches of His glory, to be strengthened with might by His Spirit in the inner man; that Christ may dwell in your hearts by faith; that you, being rooted and grounded in love, may be able to comprehend with all saints what is the breadth and length and depth and height, and to know the love of Christ which passes knowledge, that you might be filled with all the fullness of God." (Ephes. 3:14-19)

Philippians 1:9-11

"And this I pray, that your love may abound yet more and more in full knowledge and in all perception; that you may distinguish between things that differ, that you may be sincere and without offense until the day of Jesus Christ, being filled with the fruits of righteousness through Jesus Christ, to the glory and praise of God." (Philippians 1:9-11)

Colossians 1: 9 & 10

"I do not cease to pray for you, and to ask that you may be filled with the knowledge of His will, in all wisdom and spiritual understanding, that you may have a walk worthy of the Lord, fully pleasing Him, being fruitful in every good work and increasing in the knowledge of God." (Colossians 1: 9 & 10)

1 Thessalonians 3:11-13

"Now may our God and Father himself, and our Lord Jesus, direct our way to you; and may the Lord make you increase and abound in love to one another and to all men, as we do to you, so that He may establish your hearts unblamable in holiness before our God and Father, at the coming of our Lord Jesus with all his saints." (I Thessalonians 3:11-13)

2 Thessalonians 1:11-12

"Therefore we also pray always for you that our God would count you worthy of this calling and fulfill all the good pleasure of His goodness and the work of faith with power, that the name of our Lord Jesus Christ may be glorified in you, and you in Him, according to the grace of our God and the Lord Jesus Christ." (2 Thessalonians 1:11-12)

2 Thessalonians 3:1-5
"Finally, my brothers, pray for us, that the word of the Lord may have free course and be glorified, even as it is with you. And pray that we may be delivered from unreasonable and wicked men; for all do not have faith. But the Lord is faithful, who shall establish you and keep you from evil. And we have confidence in the Lord regarding you, that you both do and will do the things, which we command you, and may the Lord direct your hearts into the love of God, and into the patience of Christ." (2 Thessalonians 3:1-5)

Appendix 4

Some Favorite Life Changing Prayers

A Prayer Base On Ephesians 1:16-20

Father of Glory, give me

- a spirit of wisdom and revelation
- through a fuller knowledge of Yourself.
- Enlighten the eyes of my understanding
- to know the hope of Your calling and
- the exceeding greatness of Your power in me -(the same mighty power which your exercised in raising Christ from the dead and set Him at Your right hand in heavenly places far above all principality and power and might and dominion and every name that is named in this world and in the world to come.) (Ephesians 1:16-20)

Ephesians 3:14-19

Father, from the wealth of your glory:

- Strengthen me with might by Your Spirit in the inner man;
- that Christ may dwell in My heart by faith;
- that I may be rooted and grounded in love

- and able to comprehend (with all the saints)
- the breadth, and length and depth and height;
- and experience the love of Christ, which passes knowledge,
- and be filled with the complete fullness of God.

The Prayer Of Jabez That God Granted (1 Chronicles 4:10)

Oh that you would
- *bless me indeed*
- *and enlarge my territory*
- *that Your hand would be upon me,*
- *and that You would keep me from evil*
- *that I may not cause pain.*

A Prayer Based On Matt. 22:37

Lord pour into my heart, through the Holy Spirit, fresh love
- from You for You;
- from You for Myself
- from You for everyone.

The High Priestly Blessing (Numbers 6:24-26)

- *"Yahweh bless you and keep you.*
- *Yahweh make His face shine upon you*
- *And be gracious to you;*
- *Yahweh lift up His countenance upon you*
- *And give you peace."*

Binding Evil Spirits (Based on James 4:7 and 1 Peter 5:9)

I command all foul spirits that seek to oppress my life directly or through others to cease from all your maneuvers against me, in the Name of the Lord Jesus Christ.

Calling On The Holy Spirit (Based on Gal. 5:22)

Holy Spirit, form the
- attitudes of my heart before I have them,
- the thoughts of my mind before I think them,
- the words of my mouth before I take them
- and the steps of my feet before I take them.

A Prayer Based On 1 Thess. 5:23

Lord, keep me blameless in spirit, in soul and in body before You, and keep me humble simple and pure.

Prayer Based On Matt. 18: & Ephesians 2:10

Lord, I bind myself to You, to Your will and to the destiny and good works you have for me. I loose myself from anything that is contrary to Your will, plan and purpose for my life.

A Prayer Based On Romans 12:2

Lord, I present myself to You to be Your disciple and I give myself to You to be an agent of

Your love and mercy on the earth. I ask you to be all, in all, in all I do. Love through my heart; speak through my lips; touch through my hands; and walk this earth in my body.

A Prayer Based On Corinthians 1:31

Jesus, be my wisdom, righteousness, sanctification and redemption. May Your wisdom direct me, Your righteousness keep me, and Your redemption make me whole.

A Prayer Based on Genesis 12:3; 24:1 & Gal. 3:31

I thank You Lord, that the blessings of Abraham are on My life and that through Jesus' atoning sacrifice all curses are removed from my life and I am blessed in all things. I draw unto myself Your blessing on my spirit, my mind, my emotions my body, my finances and all the work of my hands. Make me a tremendous blessing to my generation.

A Prayer Based on John 14:12 7 John 17:21-23

Lord I present myself to You as Your disciple, to receive the glory from your Father's throne and the power of the Holy Spirit to do the works that you did, and proclaim Your message of love, truth reconciliation and mercy as You direct me.

Life Changing, World Changing Prayer

A Prayer based on Galatians 5:22 & John 4

Holy Spirit, well up within me as a fountain of life. Generate within me love, joy, peace, patience, kindness, goodness, gentleness, faithfulness, self-control, generosity, cheerfulness prayerfulness and perfect health.

A Prayer To Receive The Baptism In The Spirit (Based On Acts 1:8, 19:2 and John 14:12)

Dear Jesus, I give myself to you for Your purposes. I want my life to be used by You as an instrument and agent of Your love, mercy and Good News to the world. I do not have the power for this. I ask you now to baptize me mightily with the Holy Spirit and with power. Holy Spirit come upon me with all your gifts and graces. Give me a spirit of love and compassion, power and might, boldness and utterance, faith and humility, revelation and understanding. I receive you now from the hands of Jesus as my Enabler to live a life dedicated to You and to Your kingdom. I will pray in tongues, as you give me the ability.

(Pray this prayer in an attitude of receptivity only if you have sincerely given your life to the Lord to be an agent of His Kingdom.)

A Prayer To Receive Eternal Life
(Based On 2 Cor. 5:17-21; Rom. 5:1; Rom 12:9-11)

Father God, I come to You to be reconciled with You, and to receive eternal life.

I thank You that You have provided atonement for my sins through the death and resurrection of Jesus, Your Son. I believe that on the cross He took the blame, shame and penalty of my sin and made atonement for me so that I could be reconciled with You.

I accept your forgiveness and in return forgive others for whatever wrong they have done against me.

I lay down at the Cross the selfish, sinful side of my nature and I receive Your Spirit into my heart as a new source of love and upright living.

I ask You, Jesus, to be the Lord and Managing Director of my life and I resolve to live by Your way as you empower me by Your Spirit

As I formally release my faith in what You have done for me on the cross, I believe that I am reconciled, my sins are forgiven and that I am restored to the love and blessing of God, My Father.

To Order More copies of
Life Changing World Changing Prayer
write to Reconciliation Outreach
P.O. Box 2778, Stuart, FL 34995
Or e-mail: paulandnuala@bellsouth.net
Or by going on line to
www.reconciliationoutreach.net

You can help us with our ministry of good news by making sure that your local Christian bookstore carries these books and other books by Paul& Nuala O'Higgins

Other Books by Paul & Nuala O'Higgins
• Christianity Without Religion
• The Supernatural Habits Of The Spirit Empowered Believer
• Good News In Israel's Feasts
• New Testament Believer's & The Law
• The Four Great Covenants
• In Israel Today With Yeshua
• Have You Received The Holy Spirit?
• Life Changing World Changing Prayer

About The Authors

Paul and Nuala O'Higgins are natives of Ireland who reside in Stuart Florida. They are the directors of Reconciliation Outreach – a ministry of teaching and interdenominational evangelism.

In full-time ministry together since 1977 they have ministered in over thirty nations. Nuala's degree is in education and Paul's degrees are in Philosophy and Theology. He holds a doctorate in Biblical Theology.

They are heralds of the love of God made available by the cross. Their call is to make known the treasures of God's kingdom and equip believers to be more effective followers of Jesus.

Life Changing, World Changing Prayer

41962680R10062

Made in the USA
Charleston, SC
16 May 2015